Original title:
A Brooch in the Storm

Copyright © 2025 Creative Arts Management OÜ
All rights reserved.

Author: Colin Harrington
ISBN HARDBACK: 978-1-80586-072-3
ISBN PAPERBACK: 978-1-80586-544-5

The Light of Adornment

In chaos, it shines bright,
A sparkle in the fright.
It dances with the breeze,
Like squirrels in the trees.

A glimmer on the dress,
It seems to love the mess,
With every twist and turn,
More twirls it seems to learn.

Emblem of the Unyielding

Twirling 'round like a top,
It refuses to just stop.
Through winds that howl and bite,
It sparkles with delight.

A rebel in a gale,
Dressed like a true, bold tale.
Laughing at the rain's squall,
It stands, the life of all.

Breach of the Stormy Veil

A wink amid the squall,
Feigning it won't fall.
With confidence so grand,
It prances on the sand.

When everything goes south,
It grins without a pout.
The storm itself does cease,
To marvel at its peace.

Through the Whirlwind's Gaze

In the eye, it does sway,
Laughing storms away.
With style, it strikes a pose,
Like petals on a rose.

Unfazed by the tempest's roar,
It welcomes—oh, what's more—
A touch of madness near,
That brings with it good cheer.

Tranquil Amidst the Turmoil

In chaos, I sit, quite serene,
With snacks all around, what a scene!
The wind may howl, the rain may pound,
But here with my chips, joy is found.

Umbrellas flying, a sight so grand,
Dodging raindrops with popcorn in hand.
The world may spin, but I'll just grin,
Dancing in puddles, oh where to begin!

Threads of Grace in the Gale

In gusts of wind, I twirl and sway,
My hair's a mess, what can I say?
Fashion tips from nature's hand,
Who needs a stylist? I'm in demand!

With every step, my hat takes flight,
Chasing it down feels just so right.
Threaded stars in the tempest bright,
I laugh at fate; it's quite the sight!

Glittering Against the Abyss

In shadows cast by clouds above,
I sparkle like a treasure trove.
The rain may try to steal my shine,
But with my sequins, I'm feeling fine!

Each droplet's a dance on my cheek,
With every twirl, I cheekily peak.
Glitter and giggles fill the air,
Storms can't drown this joyous flare!

A Stalwart Sparkle

When thunder rumbles, I don't fear,
I strut with glee, full of cheer.
Each flash of light, a wink from fate,
I've got this storm, it's really great!

Raindrops tap like a merry beat,
I twirl in puddles, oh so sweet.
With laughter loud and spirits high,
A stalwart sparkle, let's fly, oh my!

The Crystal's Stand Against Chaos

In a world where raindrops dive,
A crystal twinkles, feeling alive.
The wind it howls, oh what a joke,
Yet here it sits, not even broke.

Sailboats tipping, people scream,
But our gem sparkles, a laugh it seems.
Caught in whirlwinds, like a champ,
Shining bright, it stands, a lamp.

Amidst the chaos, dancing flair,
The crystal grins without a care.
While umbrellas flip and hats take flight,
It happily twirls in pure delight.

So let the storm rage, let it shout,
This sparkling gem won't twist or pout.
With every gust, a jest it finds,
In the tempest, laughter binds.

Glisten Beneath Howling Winds.

Glisten, glimmer, what a sight,
Under clouds that love to bite.
The wind comes howling, loudest cheer,
While our jewel sways without a fear.

Trees are flapping, birds take flight,
Yet our trinket shines so bright.
Sending winks to thunder's roar,
Who knew chaos could bring such lore?

Raindrops rumble, they want a dance,
The bauble sways, a lucky chance.
With every drip, it sparkles, beams,
While stormy weather makes odd dreams.

Laughing loudly at nature's show,
Our gem just grins, puts on a glow.
Through swirling winds and splashing rain,
It seems, my friend, we're all insane!

Whispers of Resilience

In the wind's uproar, a tender giggle,
Our gem stands proud, begins to wiggle.
Whispers of laughter twist in the air,
While chaos rumbles without a care.

The world's in motion, but it won't break,
A tiny gem laughing at its wake.
While lightning dashes, a dazzling prank,
This jewel of joy sits at a plank.

Raindrops dance with bubbling cheer,
Each splash a tap—can you hear?
Through the tempest, it begins to dazzle,
Life's a riddle, let's not frazzle.

So when winds howl and shadows loom,
Remember the spark amidst the gloom.
For every storm hides a funny twist,
Just like our gem, you can't resist!

Adorning the Tempest

Adorning chaos, a sight to behold,
This gem's got stories, oh so bold.
Through thunderous laughter and skies of gray,
It twirls and spins, come what may.

The rain puts on its tap-dance shoes,
While our bauble chuckles, takes a snooze.
With each gust, it waves to the dark,
Lighting up storms with a tiny spark.

Clouds look down, trying to frown,
But the jewel just spins—won't wear a crown.
With every lightning flash, there's a jest,
In the heart of the storm, it feels blessed.

Amidst the tempest, what a display,
Our little gem finds a way to play.
So when winds rave and skies enlist,
Remember to laugh; the storms can't resist!

Glistening Through the Rain

Splashes of puddles, oh what a sight,
Dancing ducks quack, taking flight.
Umbrellas twirl in a comic parade,
While snails on the sidewalk serenade.

A hat flies off with a flail and a flap,
Rain-soaked socks become quite the cap.
In this downpour, laughter prevails,
As we slip around on our squeaky trails.

Radiance in Ruin

Winds howl like a choir gone rogue,
Kites crash down in a windy vogue.
A dance of branches, a disheveled show,
While rain-soaked cats find somewhere to go.

Oh look, a squirrel on a splashy ride,
Holding tight to its nut, with nowhere to hide.
Nature's circus in a clumsy display,
Making gloom giggle in a whimsical way.

Treasures in the Tempest

Raindrops on windows, a flickering spree,
Rabbits in wellies hop with glee.
A picnic basket floats like a boat,
As ants bring the cheese, just like they wrote.

Amidst the mud, a goldfish appears,
Grinning wide, it banishes fears.
Each splash brings a chuckle, each gust, a grin,
A joyful ruckus where chaos begins.

Gilded Amidst the Grit

Muffins in mittens, the chef's little jest,
Stirring up laughter, now that's the best!
Raindrops pitter-patter, a percussive tune,
As dogs leap around like they're over the moon.

Puddles like mirrors reflect all the fun,
Crazy old hats in a wild, wet run.
Here in the muck, we find our delight,
With giggles and splashes, oh what a sight!

Radiant in Raging Winds

A twirl of fabric, oh so bold,
Dances with breezes, stories unfold.
Feathers fly high, a whimsical sight,
Laughter persists, a dizzying flight.

Umbrellas flip, a comical scene,
Chasing down hats like a movie dream.
Smiles through the chaos, a playful charm,
In gusts and giggles, we find our calm.

The Elegance of Endurance

In a whirlwind of chaos, we stand with flair,
Watching our hair, become a wild affair.
High heels like rockets, we teeter and sway,
While raindrops parade in their own ballet.

With each gust of wind, we strike a pose,
Like models in breezes, as madness flows.
Life's a grand runway, laughter the key,
In storms we find joy, can't you see?

Ornate Against the Onslaught

Jewels scattering, oh what a sight,
As pearls roll away, causing delight.
Glittering chaos, we waltz through the squall,
Tiaras fly high, we giggle through it all.

Hats zooming past like comets on fire,
"Catch that one!" we shout, fueled by desire.
Navigating puddles, we leap with a cheer,
Fashionable chaos is wonderfully near.

Gemstones in a Gale

Through gusts of laughter, we sparkle and shine,
Dancing through raindrops, the world feels divine.
A gust turns me sideways, my coat flaps wide,
But joy in the journey, we never must hide.

With each blow of wind, there's fun to be had,
Chasing lost treasures, we're never too mad.
In storms we remember, it's all in the game,
Life's a wild party; we're all just the same.

Jewels Amidst the Tempest

Behold the pin with its dance,
Wobbling like a sailor's pants.
It clings tight on a windy spree,
Claiming all the gusts with glee.

With raindrops playing hide and seek,
The brooch just laughs, oh so cheek!
It twinkles bright, a jester's flair,
While storms toss hats into the air.

Caught in a swirl, oh what a sight,
Jewelry spinning with delight.
It pirouettes, defies the squall,
A vibrant gem, despite it all.

Chasing clouds like butterflies,
This cheerful piece won't ever die.
Through thunder claps and darkened skies,
It's the boldest one, to none's surprise.

The Trinket's Resilience

Tiny sparkles through the rain,
Laughing at the tempest's bane.
It jiggles with the thunder's roar,
A lively dance on nature's floor.

Caught in chaos, it won't yield,
Inspiring joy, it won't conceal.
A charming wink, a cheeky grin,
Each gust a riddle to unwind within.

With every gale, it starts to sway,
A daring foil to clouds of gray.
Adventurous spirit, so cavalier,
This little gem knows no fear.

When the world is in a daze,
It shimmers bright, igniting praise.
Worn on coats, or hats askew,
Its laughter sparkles and rings true.

Adornments in the Gale

A lopsided gem caught in the wind,
Where gusts abound and mischief grinned.
It flies on coats like kites in flight,
Glistening jewels in a comical plight.

As umbrellas turn inside out,
The trinket giggles, no doubt.
It tumbles and jigs in playful cheer,
With every flap, it conquers fear.

When squall clouds loom and flashes strike,
It waves hello on its shaky bike.
In the middle of storms, a sight divine,
It shows that laughter can brightly shine.

So if you spot this merry piece,
Note how it dances with such ease.
A tiny hero amidst the fuss,
Reminds us joy can always trust.

Shimmering Against the Squall

A glinting charm defies the night,
As squally winds gave quite the fright.
With every twist, it brings a laugh,
The joke's on storms; it's the epitaph.

Laughter spreads like raindrops fall,
This frolicsome pin smiles through it all.
It jangles bright with some flair,
While mischievous zephyrs toss in air.

Dancing wildly, it takes the lead,
Master of fun with a heart of greed.
Each tempest just fuels its show,
As glitter falls like confetti's glow.

In storms, it finds a shining way,
To twirl like dancers on this ballet.
Through trials and bluster, it holds sway,
A beacon of cheer that won't decay.

Jewelry of Defiance

A sparkly gem in disarray,
Defying winds that dance and sway.
With all its glimmer, bold and bright,
It twirls like mad, a silly sight.

It scoffs at clouds, all grey and fierce,
A diva's laugh it seems to pierce.
While raindrops shout and thunder roars,
This jewel just winks, and laughs, and soars.

Clinging to fabric, it jigs and jives,
Like a party guest who thrives and strives.
Although the tempest rages loud,
It wears a crown, feels grand and proud.

A Gem Amidst Chaos

In turbulent times, chaos reigns,
Yet here it sits, defies the chains.
A sparkle here, a glint so mild,
A mischievous grin of a playful child.

As winds may howl and fields may bend,
This gem persists, a loyal friend.
With every tumble, it pirouettes,
A gem that laughs while thunder sweats.

It twitches, it twirls, in gusts of glee,
A prancing jewel, wild and free.
A merry dance through Nature's jest,
In stormy chaos, it's simply blessed.

Precious Trinkets in Turbulence

Amid the squall, a locket swings,
With daring charms, it twirls and sings.
A dance of diamonds through the rain,
Playing hopscotch on the window pane.

While nature rumbles, grumbles loud,
This charm just giggles, quite unbowed.
With every clash, a giggly cheer,
It's saying, "Come on! Let's spin, my dear!"

The pearls parade, a comical scene,
As they sashay through the raucous green.
In tempest's grip, they'll shine and gleam,
With every raindrop, they bravely beam.

The Anchor of Elegance

In stormy seas where whispers roam,
An anchor gleams, with style, at home.
It laughs at tempest, spins around,
In the swirling chaos, grace is found.

Courageous charms defy the night,
As winds blow past with all their might.
With every gust, it bows and bows,
A jeweled anchor, full of vows.

With dainty sparkles and flair to show,
Each wave that crashes, it steals the show.
While storms may churn and skies turn grey,
This flair stays anchored, come what may.

Cast in the Eye of the Storm

In chaos where the seagulls squawk,
Waves dance like a pigeon on a walk.
A squirrel dons a sailor's cap,
While fish gossip in a bubbling flap.

The umbrella flips, a circus fly,
As raindrops play hopscotch from the sky.
A cat with boots struts down the street,
Curly tails twirl to a wet beat.

Balloons escape on a downward gust,
Chasing each other like kids in a bust.
Drenched and gleeful, laughter rings,
Even the clouds wear funny flings.

So in this bluster, we find our cheer,
With rubber ducks marching without fear.
The wild winds twirl a tale absurd,
Our picnic's a splash, completely unheard!

A Beacon of Glistening Hope

A lighthouse blinks with a wink and a grin,
While jellybeans tumble, let the fun begin.
The tide rolls in with giggles abound,
As seahorses frolic, joy knows no bound.

Gummi bears navigate the foam,
On marshmallow rafts, they call it home.
Sailboats of candy drift on by,
As the sun shoots rainbows that almost fly.

A crab wears sunglasses, classy and bright,
Dancing on waves in the golden light.
With a splash of humor, the ocean does play,
In this quirky haven, we'll dance all day.

So let's toast to mayhem, the giggling tide,
With glitter and laughter, we'll take a ride.
Floating on whimsy, we'll bob and we'll weave,
In this zany world, how can we grieve?

Portrait of Bravery in Waves

In a boat of biscuits, we paddle with might,
Facing jellyfish monsters, oh what a sight!
With sprinkles for shields and gumdrops for bait,
We charge through the froth, so brave and so great.

A whale wearing glasses gives us a nod,
While the seagulls narrate what's utterly odd.
With laughter like thunder, we conquer the seas,
Pirates of pastry, we sail with such ease.

Our crew is a hoot, a mix of delight,
With talking parrots that squawk into the night.
An octopus juggles with fish in a flash,
Making sure our voyage is all about splash.

So on we shall sail, with cake as our prize,
In a world full of whimsy, it's laughter we prize.
For in waves of hilarity, courage we find,
As the sea sings us stories that tickle the mind.

The Luster of Loyalty

With lemons and laughter, we troop on the shore,
Bouncing on jelly with each joyful roar.
A hamster in a cape stands bold and proud,
While turned-up waves form a giggling crowd.

A dog in a scarf sniffs out all the treats,
Wagging its tail to the rhythm of beats.
Together we twirl in the tipsy fawn,
As bubbles unwrap their magical yawn.

Through squirts of the ocean, we cling to our crew,
With marshmallow friends, we make it through.
A bond wrapped in sprinkles, tightly we cling,
Each chuckle we share makes the heartstrings sing.

So here's to the laughter that always abides,
Friendship like chocolate in turbulent tides.
With smiles as our armor, we bravely will roam,
Finding treasure in jest, our forever home.

The Ornament of the Brave

In the tempest of life, I wore a flair,
A dainty trinket, risky, yet rare.
The wind laughed, my hat took a flight,
Chasing the clouds, oh what a sight!

Each gust a giggle, a dance in the air,
My brooch became proud, with not a care,
It twinkled and jiggled, a gleeful jest,
For in storms, it's the bold that are blessed.

Marks of Valor in the Wind

With each honk of the horn, a raucous cheer,
My badge flapping wildly, oh dear, oh dear!
It twisted and turned, like a kite in the blue,
Who knew bravery looked so silly too?

A twirl of my brooch, the crowd broke to laugh,
Against nature's might, I took my own path.
In storms we find madness, a tickle and tease,
Victory's laughter is the best kind of breeze.

Luminous in the Wilds

Amongst the branches, I wore my bright gem,
It sparkled and shone like a cheeky diadem.
The squirrels took note, they couldn't resist,
Twirling around, they joined in the twist.

In the midst of the rain, it shone like a star,
While I slipped and fell, in my white rubber car.
But with giggles and grins, we danced on our way,
In nature's wild storm, we refused to dismay.

Resilience Adorned in Beauty

When the thunder grumbled, I stood with flair,
Dressed up all fancily, without a care.
Drizzles of laughter, in puddles I splashed,
Drenched but determined, my spirit was dashed.

Then came a gust, my hair flew like mad,
I sparkled in chaos, oh wasn't it glad?
So here's to the storms, the frolicsome fright,
In the heart of wild winds, we find pure delight.

Glitter in the Eye of the Hurricane

A whirlwind danced in a sparkly dress,
Twirling round trees, causing quite the mess.
With a face so bright and a laugh that was loud,
It spun like a top, drawing quite the crowd.

Umbrellas flew like kites in the air,
People squealed, with winds tousling their hair.
While rain played the drums on a rooftop stage,
The party went on, defying the rage.

The eye of the storm wore a crown of bling,
A disco ball swinging, ready to swing.
The raindrops were beats to a melody wild,
As nature laughed, like a mischievous child.

And when it was done, folks gasped in surprise,
A soaking wet revelry blinked from their eyes.
In laughter, they looked, forgetting their fright,
A hurricane's dance turned a storm into light.

Ornate Refuge from the Tempest

In a cozy nook, far from thunder's boom,
Sat a cat in a hat, with a penchant for gloom.
He sipped on some tea, while the winds like to yell,
Claiming this spot as his own, twist and swell.

A teapot depicted a fierce dragon's roar,
While cookies adorned with rainbows galore.
The velvet curtains fluttered, just for fun,
As he laughed at the storm, 'This can't be undone!'

And every light flickered, in harmony bright,
Illuminating shadows that danced with delight.
The storm might be wild, but here it was grand,
With a cat in a hat who'd a party well planned.

Whispers of thunder couldn't break up the cheer,
As long as his cookies were fresh and near.
The tempest could howl, and blast through the night,
But he'd brew up good vibes that were pure and bright.

Hushed Whispers of a Storm's Fury

The clouds were a gossip, spread thin in the sky,
As winds told tales with a dramatic sigh.
Lightning crackled, like a whispered delight,
While raindrops were dancers, in fast-paced flight.

In puddles of laughter, reflections did sway,
Each splash a snicker, come what may.
Umbrellas in hand, they turned into boats,
As people all laughed, and forgot their throats.

Each bolt that did shine resembled a wink,
In the chaos outside, they couldn't help think.
How funny these storms had a personality,
Like nature decided to throw a grand gala, you see.

With giggles and dances, they welcomed the shush,
The sound of the storm did give them a rush.
In whispers and chuckles, through tempest's roar,
They found that life's storms could still bring the lore.

The Resounding Click of Survival

A button popped off in a gusty spree,
As folks stumbled by, like leaves on a spree.
One lost their shoe, another their hat,
But laughter erupted, 'Look at that!'

With a click and a clack, shoes danced in the air,
As if the winds conspired, quite beyond compare.
With whiskers on cats twitching with glee,
Nothing could ruin their whimsical spree.

A tree wobbled, then gave them a scare,
But a squirrel in denim was already there.
He swung on a branch, his acorns held tight,
With witty remarks that made things feel light.

So when storms would come and chaos take hold,
They'd gather together, young and the old.
In the resounding laughter, they'd find their way,
As the world spun around in a comical play.

Shimmering Through the Squall

Raindrops dance on my nose,
As I search for calm in chaos.
A squirrel in boots makes a splash,
While a duck wears a hat, oh so posh.

Windy whispers try to steal,
My umbrella turned into a kite.
With every gust, I lose my balance,
Laughing while I try to hold tight.

Gusts laugh loud, tickle my cheek,
While puddles become my stage.
A waltz with a puddle, what a treat,
In nature's stormy, silly page.

Though the skies may grumble and roar,
I embrace the wild, ridiculous flair.
For in this storm, I see the truth,
Life's a jest, if you dare to care.

Beauty Beneath the Deluge

Umbrellas bloom in the wind's embrace,
A rainbow of colors, all out of place.
Rubber ducks float past, quite awry,
In torrents of laughter as I stroll by.

With each splash, a giggle erupts,
As I dodge puddles like sneaky pups.
The flowerpots dance while I grimace,
Yet nature knows how to color my face.

Raincoats don't lend much protection,
From splashes that spark pure affection.
A muddy mess becomes art anew,
In this swirling, laughing brew.

Amidst the deluge, I find delight,
In the chaos, there's joy in sight.
Who knew a storm could bring such cheer?
Under the clouds, the fun is near.

Gracing the Gales

The roof sings a tune in the gusty breeze,
As leaves pirouette like they're in the seas.
A wind chime clinks, oh so out of tune,
While I'm half a soggy sandwich by noon.

Wigs twirl past, caught by the gale,
A hat flies off like a ship bound to sail.
The trees giggle, they know this play,
As I wrestle my socks in puddles today.

Clothing becomes a waterlogged dress,
Laughing too hard, I must confess.
The wind teases my hair into frights,
But I twirl and prance for the stormy sights.

Caught in the whirl, we're having grand fun,
As honeybees buzz in the gloom of the sun.
With storms above, laughter's my aim,
In nature's wild dance, I'm winning the game.

A Spark in the Maelstrom

Lightning flickers, a mischievous tease,
The storm plays tricks, oh how it pleases.
A cat in a raincoat meows with flair,
While puddles mirror the skies' wild hair.

Clouds rumble like an orchestra's beat,
As I twirl my umbrella, oh such a feat.
I slip on a banana, lands a comedic fall,
In the tempest's arms, I'm having a ball.

Dancing raindrops wink at me,
I splash in rhythm, feeling so free.
A party of giggles ensues all around,
As chaos bursts forth where joy can be found.

In torrents of laughter, I find my spark,
A jest in the tempest, igniting the dark.
With each stormy gust, I gleefully say:
Life's a wild ride, let's dance in the spray!

In the Shadows of the Squall

Raindrops tap dance on the roof,
Squirrels hoarding acorns aloof.
A gusty breeze steals my hat,
While puddles form like a giant spat.

A dog in boots, oh what a sight,
Chasing the raindrops with delight.
A rainbow forms as clouds collide,
While umbrellas twirl, oh what a ride!

Birds huddle close, gossip and squawk,
Nature's own version of a block talk.
The chaos sings, with laughter mixed,
Underneath the tempest, just tricks.

As thunder roars, I join the jest,
With slippery shoes, I try my best.
The storm may rage, but so do we,
In our silly dance, wild and free.

A Shimmering Heart's Haven

In my pocket, a paperclip,
Thoughts of whimsy in every trip.
Rainclouds burst, umbrellas crack,
Giggling as I find my way back.

A cat with boots just strolled on by,
With stylish moves, I can't deny.
Waltzing through the puddles' gleam,
Splashing color in every dream.

My hat's a boat, oh what a ride,
Sailing through storms with ducklings by my side.
Laughter echoes amidst the rain,
In this quirky, joyful lane.

So let the thunder play its tune,
We'll dance away the afternoon.
In this swirling, soggy mess,
We find the spark, we find the zest.

Charmed by the Chaos

Tea and biscuits on a cloudy day,
Laughter dances, come what may.
A spatula flies, who knew it could?
In the chaos, we feel quite good.

The skies rumble, like a playful tease,
We grab our hats like wild geese.
Chasing umbrellas that flip and swirl,
In this storm, our joy unfurled.

Flagging down ducks for a group selfie,
We laugh so hard, we can't help but dwely.
The world spins, yet we giggle loud,
In this downpour, we feel so proud.

Dance like raindrops in the breeze,
Making memories, with such sweet ease.
Let the storm pass, with giggles galore,
In the chaos, we find so much more.

Dancer in the Downpour

A twirl, a spin, in puddles wide,
With mischievous grins, we glide.
Raindrops are confetti, oh what fun!
Here in the storm, we've just begun.

Loony hats flying, socks mismatched,
Every splash is a joke that's hatched.
We leap from corner to crowded lane,
With laughter echoing against the rain.

Socks on the line, a fashion dare,
As neighbors peek, we dance with flair.
Umbrellas like shields against a foe,
In this funny fight, we steal the show.

So dance with me, let's break the norm,
In our silly world, we'll thrive and swarm.
With each raindrop, our spirits soar,
In the wild storm, can you ask for more?

The Pin That Weathered the Wind

A tiny pin with guts to spare,
Told the gusts, "I simply dare!"
It spun around, a dizzy show,
As leaves flew past, quite nice, you know.

It danced upon a scarf so bright,
Winking at clouds, oh what a sight!
With flirty flips, it took a stand,
While twisters giggled, quite unplanned.

It threaded needles through the air,
With fashion flair beyond compare.
In chaos, it found such delight,
A brave little pin, a true light flight!

So here's to pins who boldly boast,
When storms arrive, they're on their post!
Laughing at winds, we cheer for you,
Our stylish friend, so strong and true!

Baroque Beauty in Turbulence

In tempest's grip, a brooch did shine,
With curves so bold, it crossed the line.
A swirl of jewels, like a wild dance,
As thunder rumbled, it took its chance.

It laughed at nature's fierce embrace,
With a wink and twist, it found its place.
Each raindrop sparkled like a wink,
This brooch held strong, it wouldn't sink!

As winds would howl and skies turned gray,
This beauty strutted, come what may.
With splendor grand, it swayed and swirled,
A statement piece in a stormy world!

So raise a toast to this dazzling sight,
That faced the tempest with pure delight!
For in the chaos, it still belonged,
A baroque beauty, wild and strong!

Dazzling Defiance of Nature

When storm clouds grumbled overhead,
A speckled jewel felt quite well-fed.
With dainty charms, it took a leap,
In rain's embrace, it found its cheek.

A flash of color, like a bluff,
Dared the winds, "Is this enough?"
It twinkled bright, a lively sight,
Through stormy lulls, it danced with might!

And all the raindrops cheered it on,
As puddles formed and candles shone.
With laughter bold, it faced the squall,
Defying nature, it held its thrall.

This jewel, dear friends, will never fade,
For in the tempest, boldness is made.
So let the storm roll in with flair,
A dazzling spirit, beyond compare!

A Gem's Stand Against the Maelstrom

Amidst the storm, a gem so proud,
Stood bright and bold, above the crowd.
With glimmers fierce, it dared to beam,
A tiny warrior, living the dream.

It juggled rain like a circus act,
With every drop, it struck back!
A hat tip here, a twirl and twist,
In chaos, it couldn't be missed!

As winds would whip and lightning flash,
This gem just laughed, a spirited clash.
It wore the storm like a festive gown,
No waterworks could take it down!

So here we stand, in laughter's glow,
To gems who face the winds that blow!
For in the tempest, they find their song,
A steadfast buddy, where hearts belong!

The Jewel of Serenity

In chaos wrapped, a gem so bright,
It sparkles bold, a silly sight.
With winds that howl, the rain does pour,
This jewel laughs, and wants to soar.

It rides the waves of mania's thrill,
Doing pirouettes, defying still.
While others hide, this gem will dance,
In tempest's hand, it finds romance.

Laughter echoes, and the skies may frown,
But watch it shine, won't let it drown.
A gem in jest, amidst the plight,
It twinkles bright, oh what a sight!

So when you face a wild dark jest,
Think of the gem and join the fest.
In every storm, find joy anew,
Be like that jewel, just shine on through!

Clusters of Courage

In a whirlwind's grasp, a group takes hold,
They waddle through, oh so bold!
With feathers bright, and quirky tunes,
They strut their stuff beneath the moons.

Each cluster cheers, as thunder rumbles,
Their tiny feet, skip through the tumbles.
In puddles deep, they splatter around,
With giggles loud, they dance unbound.

Oh, what a mess, this stormy game,
But clusters laugh; they take no blame.
For every drop that dares to fall,
They pirouette, and have a ball!

So when life's gusts come howling near,
Join these clusters, banish fear.
With courage found in silly rigs,
You'll face the storm and do a jig!

A Fluttering Heart in Fury

In tempest's breath, a flutter flies,
A silly heart, it never sighs.
With wings of hope, it flits about,
In roughest winds, it shows no doubt.

It zigzags through the thunder's roar,
With every flap, it dares to soar.
Who knew that storms could bring such fun?
This fluttering heart won't be outdone!

It dodges raindrops, doing flips,
With every drop, it laughs and quips.
While others cower, it takes a stand,
A silly heart, so out of hand!

So if you find a storm so wild,
Remember the heart, so free, so styled.
For in the fury, joy can bloom,
A fluttering heart dispels the gloom!

Dazzle Against the Deluge

With raindrops falling like confetti bright,
A dazzle shines, a laugh in flight.
It twirls and spins, like a circus star,
Defying the deluge, it says, "Ha, ha!"

Each splash that lands, brings giggles bold,
The dance of droplets, a sight to behold.
In slippery shoes, we slide and glide,
As storms throw tantrums, we're filled with pride.

A whimsical shimmer fights the grey,
With every bounce, we chart our way.
For laughter sparkles in puddles wide,
And joy stands tall, with arms open wide.

So dance beneath the tempest's plea,
Dazzle brightly, wild and free.
In every storm, find joy refined,
A dazzle bright, pure and unconfined!

Shattered Serenity in the Squall

A diamond danced in the tempest keen,
Like a disco ball trying to glean.
The raindrops laughed, took aim with glee,
While I ducked low beneath a tree.

A pendant swung, a windy whir,
Caught on my collar, how absurd.
The squirrels chuckled, the branches twirled,
While my hairdo laughed at the world.

A storm shaped chaos, yet oh so bright,
Bling went sliding, a comical sight.
With every gust, I felt so grand,
As jewels took flight and went off to band.

I'll treasure this mess, 'neath leaves and skies,
A whirlwind tale, with twinkling cries.
So if you see my treasure fly,
Rest assured, it's just the storm's sly hi!

The Locket That Braved the Tide

A locket swung on my neck so tight,
Which whispered secrets in the night.
But then a wave came with a sense of spite,
And suddenly, it took off in flight!

The ocean gurgled with a clanking tune,
As necklaces danced beneath the moon.
And I stood there, soaked, in a monsoon,
Wishing for dry land, oh for a boon!

But pearls were rolling like marbles in play,
Gathering shells in their stylish fray.
A sea anemone gave a cheeky sway,
Inviting my jewels to join the ballet.

I chuckled softly, despite my wet plight,
For even the sea has a sense of light.
With each wave crashing, the world felt right,
As laughter echoed into the night.

Echoes of Elegance in Hardship

In a ruffled gown and a wayward hat,
I tripped on the rug, oh how I spat!
The chandelier winked, 'How clumsy is that?'
While my brooch took flight, like a clever brat.

It skittered across polished wood so grand,
Gleaming and gliding, it made its own stand.
While I chased after, a fan in my hand,
Slipping and sliding, oh this wasn't planned!

The butler looked on, a smile he wore,
As my jewels played tag on the ballroom floor.
With each little crisis, I welcomed more,
For laughter and chaos made my heart soar.

So who needs decorum in this wild dance?
When even the jewels crave a chance.
I'll embrace this mishap, oh take a glance,
As elegance blooms from a clumsy prance!

The Cufflink's Vigil in Fury

A cufflink stood firm amid the storm,
Braving each raindrop, an odd little form.
'Oh, how ridiculous!' it did transform,
As I searched frantically to keep it warm.

The jacket flapped like a flag in fear,
While puddles splashed with laughter near.
My cufflink winked, 'No need for a tear,'
'Let's charm this chaos, for fun is here!'

The wind howled tales of dapper chic,
I rolled in puddles, didn't feel meek.
With every laugh, my attire was unique,
As my accessories joined in, bold and bleak.

So here's to the storm, the cufflink's own glee,
Embracing mischief, wild and free.
With twinkling wit, the tempest can see,
That fashion's a riot, even in debris!

Brilliance Amidst the Whirlwind

In a gale of chaos, I twirl and spin,
With my sparkly pin, I just can't win.
Dancing with raindrops, how silly I seem,
But hey, who cares? I'm living the dream!

The winds may howl, but I stand my ground,
With glittery flair, I'm joyfully bound.
Ribbons of laughter flutter and sway,
As I glide through the storm in a dazzling display.

Why frown when you can wear beads in your hair?
Each gust a reminder to play without care.
The clouds can grumble, but it's all in good fun,
I'll shine like a beacon, till the bad weather's done!

So bring on the chaos, I'll take it in stride,
With sparkles and giggles, I relish the ride.
In storms and in squalls, with a wink I'll resist,
Who knew that a storm could be such a twist?

Shielded by Sapphire and Storm

Hiding from raindrops, beneath a grand hat,
With gems and with laughter, I'm all about that!
The sky is a painter, with splashes of gray,
But I'm strutting my bling, come what may!

Oh, the thunder may rumble, but I won't lose cheer,
For my trusty blue jewel makes worries unclear.
Hail may come down like an uninvited guest,
Yet I smile through it all, for I'm fabulously dressed!

Each gust is a tickle, each splash just a laugh,
I'll twirl like a dervish, take storm as my staff.
When lightning strikes, I just strike a pose,
Who knew Mother Nature could use some new clothes?

So here's to the tempest, with a wink and a cheer,
I'm simply untouchable, with darling flair near.
In jewels and in laughter, I'll revel and play,
For sapphire dreams shine bright on stormy days!

Memory's Spark Against the Darkness

In shadows so dim, where giggles retreat,
A spark lights the way, creating a beat.
With trinkets and tales from the days of yore,
I'll laugh in the face of dark, that's my score!

Each memory glimmers, like stars in the night,
With whimsy and fun, I'll fuel up my light.
The clouds can be grumpy; they don't know my name,
I'll tickle the gloom with my playful little game.

From baubles to gossip, my treasures run deep,
The laughter resounding makes shadows not keep.
I'll dance with nostalgia, oh sweet but absurd,
For life's a grand joke, and I'm not quite unheard!

So in stormy moments, when past seems to call,
I'll wear my bright memories, stand fun and tall.
Against the dark whispers, I shine like a gem,
With humor and spark, I'll always condemn!

Caught Between Lightning and Love

In a twinkle of love, the thunder shakes near,
Between sparks of romance, I fumble in fear.
But the storm can't resist a heart full of cheer,
So I laugh as I juggle my hopes and my sneers!

Oh love, it's a dance on this slippery floor,
With lightning as backdrop, I ask for some more.
The clouds may be heavy, but my heart's light as air,
As we dive through the chaos with outrageously flair!

Every bolt brings a giggle, a new chance to play,
We sizzle and pop, come what may, come what may!
With jokes like our raindrops, they fall into place,
Finding warmth in the storm, we're both full of grace.

Yet should the sky darken, or laughter grow thin,
We'll tether our spirits, find joy 'neath the din.
Caught between lightning, there's nothing to fear,
With love as our shield, let it rain, let it cheer!

Through the Tempestuous Dance

In gales that whirl and twirl around,
I wear mismatched socks, my feet unbound.
The wind tries hard to steal my hat,
But with a wiggle, I claim it back!

With gusty giggles in every stride,
I prance like a hero in my stormy ride.
The puddles splash, my pants are wet,
Yet in my heart, there's no regret.

As branches sway, I dance with glee,
A kite flies past, as if to flee.
With thunder's laugh and lightning's grin,
Who knew a storm could be such a win?

So here I twirl, a sight so bright,
In rain-soaked shoes, through day and night.
With every leap, a splatter is cast,
In this tempest, I'm free at last!

Enchantment Amidst the Fury

The clouds are frowning, or so they say,
Yet here I am, sillier every day.
With rubber ducks up in the air,
I wave my arms, without a care.

The winds are fierce, they try to bite,
But I'm just here for a comical fight.
With tattered cape, I run and glide,
A superhero with joy as my guide.

The road is slick, I slip and slide,
Giggling loud, I cannot hide.
Each raindrop's laugh, a tickle divine,
In fury's heart, I bring the shine.

So bring the thunder, let it roar,
While I keep dancing, who could ask for more?
In chaos' grip, I take my chance,
With lightning in my step, I prance!

The Glow of the Brave

A lantern shines within the rain,
Where bravery blooms despite the strain.
I leap through puddles, splash and spray,
   Making the storm my grand ballet.

With every gust, I raise my chin,
Drenched but bright, I cannot dim.
Singing songs of joy and cheer,
   I twirl in storms like a cavalier.

The clouds may grumble, the sky may frown,
But look at me, I'll never drown!
With laughter loud, I make my stand,
   A glow of courage in this land.

From thunder's clap to nature's song,
I steal the show, all day long.
So let the tempest roar and rave,
I shine with laughter, oh so brave!

The Jewel of Perseverance

The wind may howl, but I won't flee,
With a smile wide, I find my glee.
Each raindrop's dance, a silly beat,
In stormy trials, I will not retreat.

I wear my raincoat, a fabulous sight,
With polka dots, oh what a delight!
While others shiver, I'm all aglow,
Dancing my way through the rainy show.

The storm may try to steal my cheer,
Yet with every howl, I bring good cheer.
I'll wear my shadows like a crown,
Turning each frown upside down.

So here I stand, my spirit bright,
In the grip of chaos, hearts take flight.
With every storm, I find my way,
A jewel of joy, come what may!

Emblems of Hope in Chaos

A bird with a bowler hat,
Danced in the downpour, what's that?
Umbrellas turned inside out,
Laughter muffled in the sprout.

The rain played music on the street,
Where puddles formed a quirky beat.
A cat in galoshes pranced around,
While chaos wore a silly crown.

In the whirlwind, a kite went rogue,
Tangled in ribbons, it did a vogue.
A dog wore goggles, ready to surf,
As life turned topsy-turvy on earth.

With every splash, a chuckle grew,
Finding joy in each gust that blew.
So in the tempest, let's rejoice,
For every storm gives us a voice.

A Treasure Under Duress

Amid the thunder, a spoon found fame,
Swirling in whirlwinds, oh what a game!
A squirrel with boots, quite the brave show,
Making a splash, not caring to flow.

Cups and saucers took a wild ride,
In the eye of the storm, they surely abide.
An apple rolled by with a grin so wide,
Said, "When life gets rocky, let's not slide!"

A hat flew off, went up in a tree,
While a fish in a bowl yelled, "Look at me!"
Under duress, they dance and twirl,
Each mishap a metaphor, life's a whirl.

So here we stand, amid nature's jest,
Finding gold in chaos, oh what a quest!
With laughter our treasure, we'll never regret,
Embracing the mess, we're all set.

Diadems Beneath Darkened Skies

A crown of daisies pranced on the wind,
While clouds had a wrestling match, chagrined.
Lollipop trees swayed without a care,
As raindrops giggled, splashing everywhere.

Rainbows seemed to play peekaboo,
With unicorns sharing giggly views.
Funny shoes flew past on a whim,
It rained surprises, so life wouldn't dim.

Jellybeans tossed from high above,
Created a feast that all would love.
Stormy skies couldn't dampen the cheer,
As laughter sparkled, drawing us near.

Diadems glistened in the light of jest,
Amongst the clouds, we found our fest.
For in every storm, humor will bloom,
Turning chaos to laughter, banishing gloom.

The Resilience of a Singular Jewel

A lonely gem danced in the rain,
Winking at clouds, ignoring the pain.
Amidst the flurry, it spun in delight,
Saying, "Bring on the chaos, I'll be alright!"

A rubber duck sailed past in a rush,
Waving at pillows that floated, no hush.
Through windstorms and whirls, it holds its place,
With every splash, a grin on its face.

In the eye of the tempest, laughter emerged,
As frogs in tuxedos joyously surged.
No hurdle too high, no puddle too deep,
With silly antics, we joyfully leap.

So here's to the jewel, steadfast and bright,
In a sea of madness, a heart filled with light.
For when skies get stormy, we must remember,
That joy's the true treasure, glowing like ember.

Artistry Anchored in Agitation

In chaos, paint flies wild, ahoy!
A canvas made of laughter, a ploy.
Brushes dance like leaves in a gale,
Creating smiles, where dreams set sail.

Mismatched colors, oh what a scene!
Dancing ducks in a cotton candy sheen.
The artist trips, the world gives a cheer,
Masterpieces born from chocolate smears.

In the whirlwind, we find a rhyme,
Every stumble turns into prime time.
Comedy storms through the studio door,
And artistry thrives, forever more!

What fun it is to jest and tease,
As brushes yank with clamorous ease.
In the mess, we embrace a grin,
And agitation becomes our kin.

Radiance Rising from Ruin

Oh, what a mess this kitchen's become,
Spaghetti scattered, a culinary sum.
Tomato splatters, a pizza fight,
Dinner chaos makes every night bright!

With pots and pans in a gleeful dance,
Mistakes become a gourmet chance.
In the wreckage, flavors take flight,
Burnt garlic turns into pure delight.

The oven's smoking, I gasp and chortle,
A burnt soufflé? Now that's a novel!
Yet through the ruin, we find our glow,
Radiant laughter in the after-show.

Amidst the mess, a feast we find,
Cooking's a riot—a jester, not blind.
Every flop, a story to tell,
In radiant ruins, we laugh so well!

The Guarded Glow of Fragile Things

She carries teacups like her secrets dear,
Dancing with care, full of cheer.
A tip, a wobble, laughter in slime,
Flush of crimson, oh, isn't it prime?

Heartbeats hidden behind fragile glass,
A collection that's bound to make one laugh.
With each little crack, a giggle unfurls,
In porcelain worlds where chaos swirls.

Her treasure chest, it tips with glee,
Petunias singing, a sided spree.
Oh, the glow of bounty and risk combined,
In delicate chaos, sweet joy we find!

So guard your heart, but let it sway,
In the slip, the stumble, we'll find our way.
A fragile thing, yet mirthfully strong,
In its glow, we always belong.

Chronicles of a Stalwart Adornment

In the alleyway, a tiara lies,
Sparkling hope beneath dreary skies.
Once a queen, now a jester's prize,
Chasing pigeons and playful cries.

Napkin rings dance at the dinner table,
Conducting chaos, a merry fable.
With each twist, we giggle and share,
Stories of shine and utter despair!

Jewels of laughter, gems of delight,
Adorning our minds like stars in the night.
From tarnished history, joy does cling,
In chronicles penned by a marigold ring.

With every twinkle, a tale unfolds,
In the ruckus, a splendid gold.
Adorned with laughter and silly knickknacks,
The stalwart charm brings chuckles back!

The Amulet of the Storm

In the chaos of rain, I found a pin,
A sparkly charm, oh where to begin!
It danced on my coat, held tight by a thread,
I laughed as it twirled while others just fled.

When the wind howled loud, and the skies turned gray,
My brooch took a stand, said, "Let's save the day!"
With a wink and a spin, it calmed all the dread,
While everyone else looked down at their bread.

Through puddles we splashed, my pin stayed so brave,
It jiggled and jived, a true glittery wave.
What joy in my heart, to wear such delight,
When the storm's lively dance felt just so right.

So here's to the jewels in blustery glee,
Who shine through the tempest and stay fancy-free!
Each twinkle a giggle, each shine brings a grin,
With charm on my lapel, I'm ready to spin!

Tranquil Treasures

In the midst of the gale, with my pin on display,
I strolled through the storm like it's just my play.
Raindrops were laughing, dancing on my nose,
While my 'gem of the storm' giggled, goodness knows!

It jangled and jingled, a true sight to see,
As I carried it proudly like a VIP.
People huddled and hid, their umbrellas awry,
While I twirled in the rain, oh, I felt like a fly!

"What's your secret?" they asked while I danced away,
I shrugged with a grin, keeping worries at bay.
With glittering smiles through the puddles I leapt,
My treasure so snazzy, not one tear I wept.

So let the storms come, with their might and their roar,
I'll wear my sweet charm and embrace the downpour!
A lesson in laughter, a twinkle, a peek,
With joy held so high, it's the strong that are chic!

The Resilient Radiance

Under dark clouds, my brooch has a say,
"It's just a bit breezy, come join in the play!"
As my friends sought cover, I shone like a star,
My sparkling companion, the best by far.

Through gusts of adventure and splashes of rain,
My pin wore its humor, danced wild with the strain.
While umbrellas flipped, like boats in a storm,
I posed for a picture, my style oh-so-warm.

Was it foolish? Some quipped, with a chuckle and tease,
But my jewelry laughed back, said, "Life's meant to please!"
We twirled in the chaos, so light and so free,
In storms, after all, we make our own glee.

So here's to the brave who shine bright in a squall,
With treasures that jingle and laughter for all.
May your joy be persistent, your sparkle spread wide,
In every bad weather, let your spirit abide!

A Tale of Tenacity

When thunder and chaos dance over the town,
I sport my fine pin, I'm never so down.
With a flick and a flair, it pulls me right through,
"Be bold!" it assures me, "You've got this, it's true!"

In puddles I waddle, not caring for fright,
As my brooch winks and glimmers, oh what a sight!
Like a lighthouse it shines, through the foggy delight,
In stormy conditions, I'm ready to kite!

The weather might roar, but my spirit's a ray,
With a twirl of my charm, I'm just here to play.
Let the rain come pouring, let wild winds entwine,
With joy in my heart, I'll forever shine.

So gather your treasures, don't shy from the squall,
For the laughter we wear is the best thing of all!
With courage we'll dance, no fear to reclaim,
Embrace the wild storms; it's part of the game!

A Token in the Tempest

Winds howl like a caffeinated cat,
Raindrops dance, wearing a hat.
Umbrellas flip, a funny sight,
As socks get soggy, what a flight!

My hair's a mess, a frizzy show,
Oh look, a duck just stole my dough!
Splashing puddles, laughter loud,
In this chaos, I feel so proud.

The clouds are grumpy, frowning low,
Yet here I stand, in rainbow glow.
A storm can't dampen silly cheer,
My heart's a beacon, bright and clear.

So let it rain, let thunder roll,
I'll dance around, in puddles, whole!
With every gust, I just embrace,
This tempest's wild and funny grace.

The Sturdy Heart's Adornment

A clattering gust sends hats a-flying,
While I just giggle, not even trying.
Sturdy heart's pinned with laughter's tack,
Holding hope, never looking back.

Puddles jump under joyful feet,
Becoming partners in this wet greet.
The skies might moan, but here I'll stand,
My charms intact, just a bit unplanned.

Raindrops like confetti in the air,
I twirl around without a care.
Sturdy heart, with glee adorned,
In tempest's midst, I'm brightly warmed.

The storm may bluster, rumble, rage,
But I'm the star upon this stage!
Dancing in chaos, a colorful spree,
Adorned by joy, wild and free.

Beneath the Thunder's Clutch

Thunder grumbles like an old man,
While lightning strikes up a silly plan.
A paper boat floats by in dread,
I see its fate and burst out in red!

The raindrops play a musical beat,
Splashing shy fish wearing boots on their feet.
I can't help but laugh, oh what a sight,
As puddles become my wading delight.

With thunder like jokes meant to chuckle,
I spin in circles, not one bit buckled.
Drenched to the bone, I take a stand,
With nature's quirks at my command.

The clouds rumble like a bad joke,
Yet here I traipse, fun never broke.
Beneath the wild, I remain unbent,
In this storm, my laughter's sent.

The Charm of Courage

Wind's a tickler, what a tease,
Making mischief with the trees.
I hold my ground, smirk on my face,
In this frolic of nature's embrace.

With each raindrop comes pogo fun,
Jumping high, I'll never run.
Courage's charm, a silly dance,
Twisting and twirling, oh what a chance!

As puddles giggle and splash around,
I strut my stuff, no fears found.
In stormy chaos, I wear a grin,
For heart's adornments always win.

So let the thunder drum a beat,
I'll tap my toes, feel the heat.
The charm of courage, bright and bold,
Shining through, as laughter unfolds.

Carved from Chaos

In the whirlwind of mess, I stand still,
A paperclip hat, my backdrop, a thrill.
Wind howls like a beast, all wild and free,
I laugh as it tosses my umbrella, whee!

Rain's a raucous jester, splashing all around,
My hair's a wet mop, it droops, it's quite profound.
But in this swirling dance of woe,
I'm a master of silliness, putting on a show!

Puddles form lakes, a swimming spot divine,
I dive in with style, it's a splashy design.
Laughter echoes loud, 'neath stormy delight,
In chaos, a joy, as the world takes flight.

Clouds frown above, but laughter will win,
In this manic moment, I twirl with a spin.
Chaos may reign, but I'll strut and parade,
For joy's my brooch, as the storm is betrayed!

Pendants of Peace in the Storm

Thunder's a drummer, keeps time with the rain,
I'm a dancing fool, shedding worry and pain.
With raindrops as pearls, I prance to and fro,
Glancing sideways at lightning, "Hey, nice show!"

Umbrellas like mushrooms, pop up in a row,
Fashion's new trend, oh what a grand flow!
Slip in the puddle, a slip-and-slide fate,
Laugh through the chaos, why not celebrate?

Windy gusts teasing, they tug on my coat,
"Catch me if you can!" My spirit's afloat.
Each splash is a giggle, each gust a dance card,
While the storm throws its tantrum, I play the wild bard.

Storm clouds can frown, but I wear a bright smile,
In my silly parade, I'll go many a mile.
So bring on the tempest, I welcome the art,
For laughter, dear friend, is the best form of heart!

An Emblem of Bravery

Dressed in my raincoat, a warrior indeed,
Armed with my gumboots, I'm ready to lead.
The storm tries to grumble, but I raise my chin,
I dance through the downpour, let the fun begin!

My umbrella's a shield, a knight's trusty lance,
I march through the chaos, all set for a prance.
With every big splash, a victory cheer,
The puddles are battlegrounds, no need to fear!

Raindrops are confetti, a festive brigade,
My heart wearing valor, I'm never dismayed.
For every loud rumble, I'll giggle and prance,
In the face of a storm, I refuse to not dance.

Bravery shines brighter than the flash of the light,
With humor as armor, I conquer the night.
So, storm, have your fun, switch on your loud show,
I'm the jester of courage, come join in the glow!

The Radiant Refuge

Amidst crashing thunder and torrential downpours,
I find cozy corners, oh, what fun outdoors!
Snug in my blanket fort, I'm safe from the roar,
Sipping hot cocoa, I couldn't ask for more.

A stormy debate, the sky fuming in gray,
While I battle marshmallows, in my warm stay.
Each crash of the sky, just my soundtrack of glee,
From this radiant refuge, I shout, "Free me!"

I watch windows warp, like a fun-house delight,
As shadows do dance with the flicker of light.
A giggle escapes me as thunder goes boom,
While I host a tea party in my cozy room.

So let the storm rattle, let the winds clash and fight,
I'm a fearless confection, a delight in the night.
Wrapped in this chaos, I find my true bliss,
In this stormy embrace, I discover my kiss!

Pendant of the Perilous Skies

In the chaos of wind, a charm takes flight,
Dancing on clouds like a comedian's delight.
It twirls through the gales, with a grin so wide,
A jester in nature, on this wild ride.

With lightning as backdrop, it performs with glee,
Singing to thunder, "Come laugh with me!"
The raindrops all giggle, they plop and they pat,
As the jewel spins 'round wearing a stormy hat.

Each gust is a tickle, each wave a fun-prank,
While umbrellas go flying in this stormy prank.
A joyful adornment on nature's mad quest,
With a wink and a laugh, it brings out the best.

A Tryst with Turbulence

A pendant swings low, caught in a breeze,
Swinging like dancers, it aims to please.
It flirts with the clouds, with a mischievous stare,
Challenging storms like it just doesn't care.

The winds try to catch it, but oh, what a show!
It twirls and it spins, with an effortless flow.
Raindrops start chuckling, as they splash in delight,
While our pendant keeps jiving through day and through night.

With a wink at the skies, it takes a bold chance,
In this turbulent dance, all the clouds break a glance.
Nature's own silly, a gem full of spark,
Laughing at chaos in the deepening dark.

Twinkling Through the Tempests

A sparkle flickers in the haze of the gray,
Wearing mischief's grin as it dances away.
Through whirlwinds it weaves, like a magpie's charm,
Wrapping the storm in its twinkling arm.

It jests with the thunder, "Come show me your might!"
Popping like popcorn when struck by the light.
The storm wears a coat made of laughter and cheer,
As the jewel keeps prancing, it knows no fear.

With droplets of joy splashing everywhere,
Nature's own folly, a gem in midair.
Twinkling through tempests, it knows how to play,
In a laughable ruckus, it leads the ballet.

Resplendent Amidst Ruin

Glinting through chaos, it basks in the fright,
A jewel on a mission, to bring pure delight.
With a chuckle it rides on the back of the squall,
Defying the storm, it gleefully calls.

While trees bend and sway, it keeps its proud stance,
Inviting the downpour for a wild chance.
"Come join the parade!" it shines with such glee,
While the world all around swoops and swirls like a spree.

In a whirlwind of laughter, it twirls like a sprite,
Even the rain wants to join in the night.
Resplendent and brave, laughing wildly at doom,
A gem in the tempest, spreading joy in the gloom.

The Stone of Strength

In a storm, I found my charm,
A rock so stout, it brought no harm.
I laughed aloud as lightning cracked,
For this old stone was never whacked.

It bounced right back, all chips intact,
With soggy shoes, I made my pact.
I'd wear it proud, a weighty friend,
In gusty gales, it had no end.

With every gust, it sparked my glee,
I danced in puddles, wild and free.
The raindrops rapped a silly tune,
And strength became my afternoon.

So if you're caught in tempest's tease,
Just take a breath and laugh with ease.
For with a stone by your side tight,
You might just find the storm is bright.

Echoes of Beauty in the Breeze

The wind declared, 'I am all style!'
With ruffled hair that made me smile.
'Look how I toss your thoughts away,
And swirl them 'round like a ballet!'

The raindrops laughed on windowpanes,
Pretending they were falling trains.
They raced each other, round and round,
While twirling leaves made joyful sound.

An umbrella flipped, a jaunty dance,
A fleeting chance, a breezy prance.
'You can't catch me, I'm far too grand!'
It spun away just like a band.

So if you hear the gusts out there,
Just drop your worries, have a flare.
In every gale, a chuckle grows,
The echoes of the breeze—who knows?

A Glittering Guardian

A shiny pin upon my coat,
It sparkles bright, like a boat afloat.
'Fear not!' it chirps in tempest's sigh,
'I'll keep you safe; just give a try!'

The wind may howl and clouds may fume,
But I stand tall; I claim the room.
With glints of light that dance around,
A guardian that won't back down!

It twirls in gales and plays the fool,
Pretending chaos is just cool.
With every flash, it seems to say,
'Embrace the storm; let's laugh away!'

So here's to pins and playful charms,
That guard us all with quirky arms.
Against the squalls, just hold them tight,
For they've got laughter in their light.

Against the Wrath of Nature

The skies erupted, 'Can you believe?'
As weather maps began to weave.
With clouds like pillows, soft yet grim,
I cracked a joke, no mood to dim.

The trees were shaking, but with grace,
They waved their branches in mad chase.
I watched them dance, a wild feat,
A nature show—how can't be beat?

The thunder grumbled, belly full,
While lightning flashed, in grand parade,
Yet here I stood, carefree and spry,
With every clap, I waved goodbye.

So when the storm spills out its might,
Just chuckle softly, hold on tight.
For in that tempest, fun is found,
In nature's wrath, we spin around.

www.ingramcontent.com/pod-product-compliance
Lightning Source LLC
Chambersburg PA
CBHW051730290426
43661CB00122B/211